WE ARE YOUNG

Words and Music by JEFF BHASKER,
ANDREW DOST, JACK ANTONOFF
and NATHANIEL RUESS

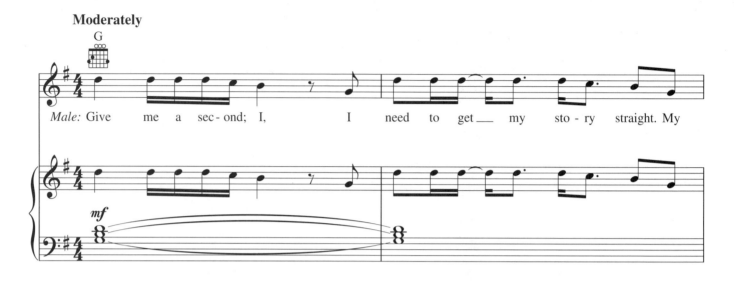

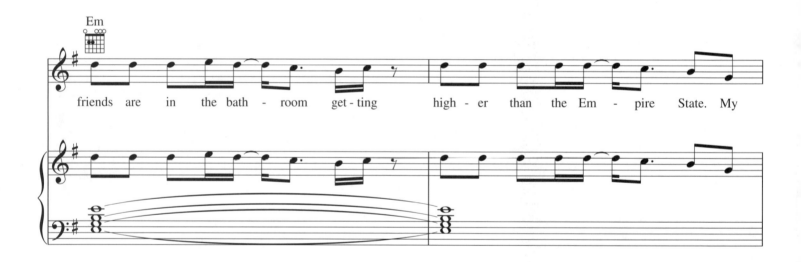

THE EDGE OF GLORY

Words and Music by STEFANI GERMANOTTA,
PAUL BLAIR and FERNANDO GARIBAY

hang - ing on a mo - ment with you. ___ I'm on the edge ___ with you. ___

I'm on the edge ___ with you. ___ I'm on the edge ___ with you.

I WON'T GIVE UP

Words and Music by JASON MRAZ
and MICHAEL NATTER

WE ARE THE CHAMPIONS

Words and Music by
FREDDIE MERCURY

SCHOOL'S OUT

Words and Music by ALICE COOPER
and MICHAEL BRUCE

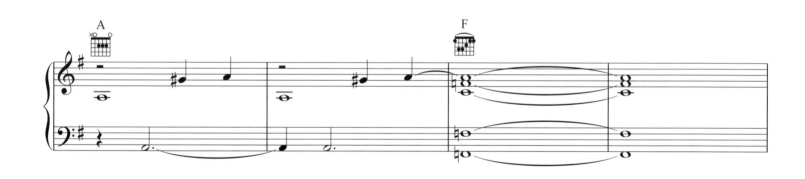

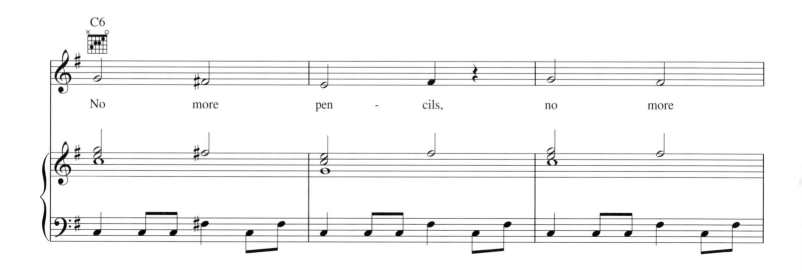

books. _____ No more teach - er's

dirt - y looks. _____

I WAS HERE

Words and Music by
DIANE WARREN

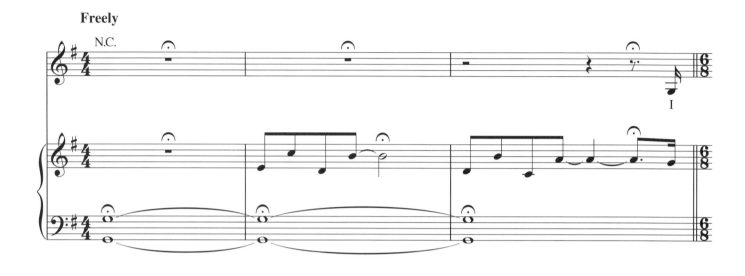

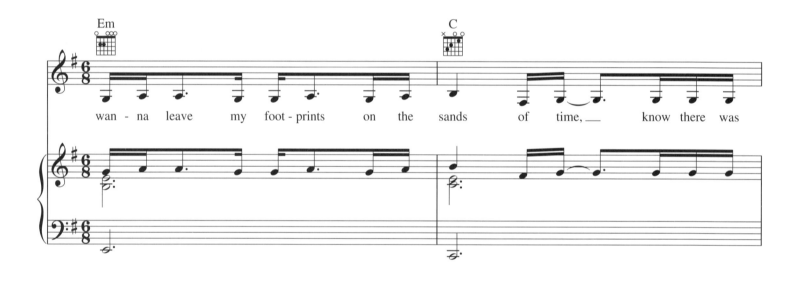

I'LL REMEMBER

Words and Music by PATRICK LEONARD,
RICHARD PAGE and MADONNA

YOU GET WHAT YOU GIVE

Words and Music by GREGG ALEXANDER
and RICK NOWELS

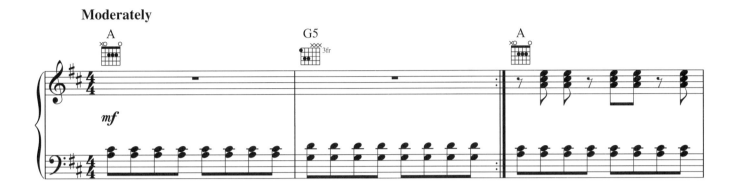

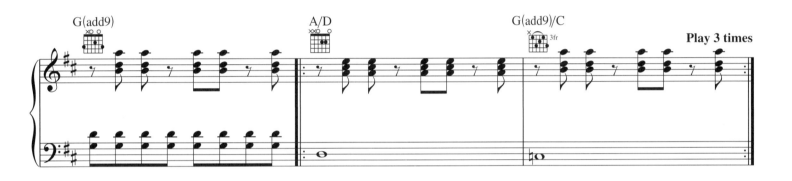

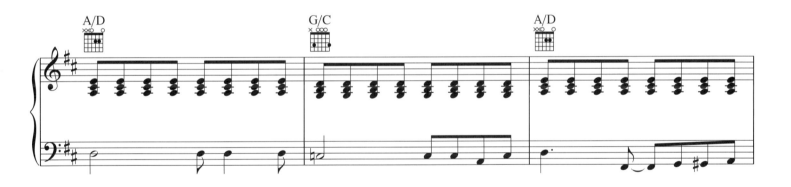

Wake up, kids. ___ We've got the dream-ers dis-ease. ___
Frien - e - mies, ___ who when you're down, ain't your friend. __
Four a. m., ___ we ran a mir-a-cle mile. ___

49

NOT THE END

Words and Music by CHUCK BUTLER
and LUKE BROWN

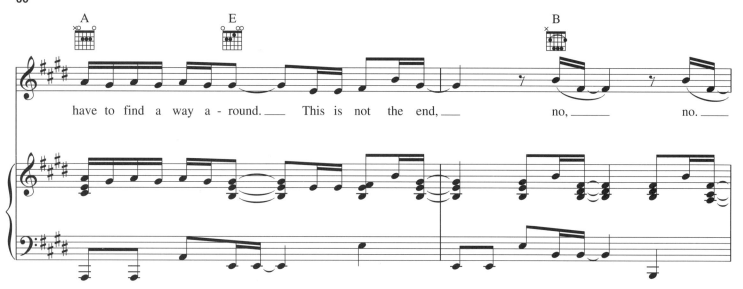

have to find a way a - round.____ This is not the end, ____ no, _____ no.____

_____ This is not the end.____

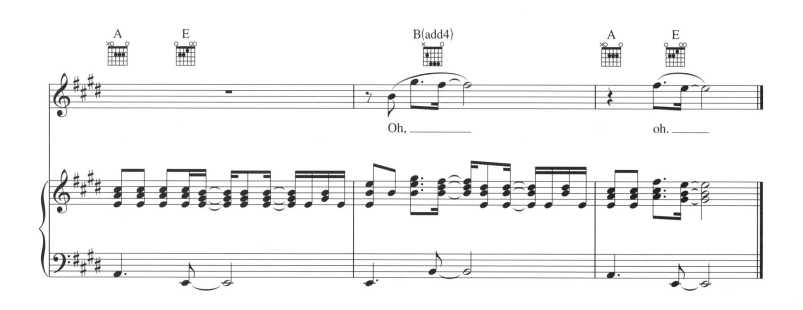

Oh, _____ oh. _____

ROOTS BEFORE BRANCHES

Words and Music by ADAM ANDERS
and NICOLE HASSMAN

Hey, yeah, hey. So

man-y things to do and say but I can't seem to find my way, but I
Some-times I don't wan-na feel and for-get the pain is real; put my

wan-na know how. I
head in the clouds. I

GLORY DAYS

Words and Music by
BRUCE SPRINGSTEEN

1. I had a friend, __ was a big base - ball play - er
2., 3. *(See additional lyrics)*

back in __ high school. __ He could throw __ that speed-

-ball by __ you, make you look __ like a fool, __ boy. __

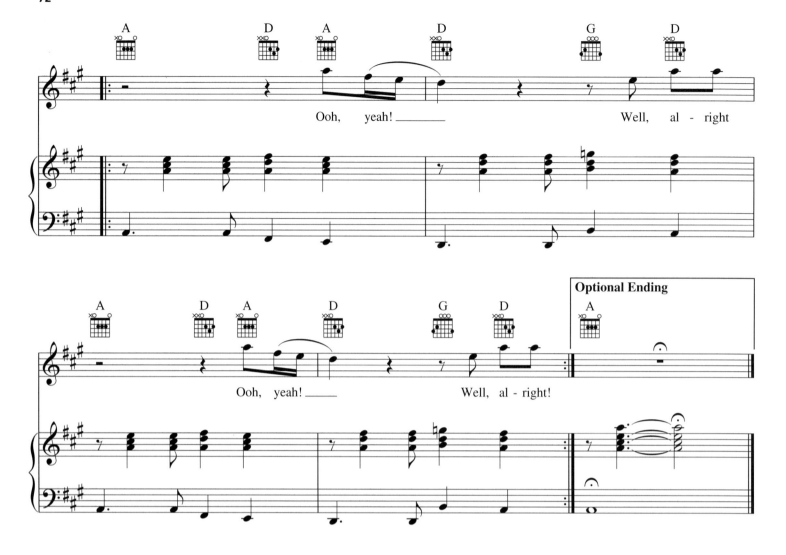

Additional Lyrics

2. Well, there's a girl that lives up the block;
   Back in school she could turn all the boys' heads.
   Sometimes on a Friday, I'll stop by and have a few drinks
   After she put her kids to bed.
   Her and her husband, Bobby, well, they split up;
   I guess it's two years gone by now.
   We just sit around and talk about the old times;
   She says when she feels like crying she starts laughin'
   Thinkin' 'bout glory days.

   Chorus

3. Think I'm going down to the well tonight,
   And I'm gonna drink till I get my fill.
   And I hope when I get old I don't sit around thinkin' about it,
   But I probably will.
   Yeah, just sittin' back tryin' to recapture
   A little of the glory of,
   Well the time slips away and leaves you with nothing', mister,
   But boring stories
   Of glory days.

   Chorus

FOREVER YOUNG

Words and Music by ROD STEWART,
KEVIN SAVIGAR, JIM CREGAN
and BOB DYLAN

Moderate Acoustic Ballad

GOOD RIDDANCE
(Time of Your Life)

Words by BILLIE JOE
Music by GREEN DAY

An - oth - er turn -
So take the pho -
Instrumental solo ad lib.

- ing point, __ a fork __ stuck in __ the __ road.
- to - graphs __ and still - frames in __ your __ mind,